FAIRACRES PUBLICATIONS 208

TIME

Archpriest Dumitru Stăniloae

Metropolitan Kallistos Ware

First Edition 2023

Fairacres Publications No. 208

Print ISBN 978-0-7283-0365-2
Fairacres Publications Series ISSN 0307-1405

Archpriest Dumitru Stăniloae: *Eternity & Time*
First published by SLG Press 1982
Second edition 2001

Metropolitan Kallistos Ware: 'Time: Prison or Path to Freedom?'
First published in *Fairacres Chronicle,* Winter 1989

Edited and typeset in Palatino Linotype by Julia Craig-McFeely

Biblical quotations are taken from the New Revised Standard Version of the Bible unless otherwise noted

SLG Press
Convent of the Incarnation
Fairacres • Oxford
www.slgpress.co.uk

Printed by
Grosvenor Group Ltd, Loughton, Essex

CONTENTS

Introduction

The first of the two texts presented here comes from a lecture given by the late Fr Dumitru Stăniloae during his second visit to Fairacres in the summer of 1971. The lecture was given in French and simultaneously translated into English by Fr Donald Allchin. Fr Dumitru was speaking not from a prepared document but from brief notes, and the text as printed here is an edited transcription of the tape-recording made on that occasion.

The lecture made a deep and lasting impression on the sisters who heard it and, twelve years after the collapse of Communism in Eastern Europe, SLG Press were able to publish it and make it more widely known in print.[1]

The end of World War II inaugurated a period of suffering and oppression for the Romanian people of which, even today, we in the West know very little. As an Orthodox theologian of great distinction Fr Dumitru was at the centre of an informal circle of intellectuals in Bucharest—writers, poets, scientists and scholars—who met to discuss the meaning of Christian faith for the period in which they were living. At the same time, through his new edition of the *Philokalia*, the great Orthodox anthology of spiritual texts, he was exercising a profound influence on the unexpected revival of monastic life in Romania. Not only his theological eminence but also his remarkable gift for friendship made him greatly loved and revered in monastic houses throughout Romania. Thus, in the 1950s, when the state intensified its persecution of churchmen and intellectuals, his arrest and imprisonment were not surprising. For five years Fr Dumitru

[1] Dumitru Stăniloae, *Eternity and Time*, trans. A. M. Allchin, Fairacres Publicatiions 136 (SLG Press, 1982, 2nd edn 2001).

was confined in one of the notorious political prisons by which the regime sought systematically to stamp out and destroy the intellectual elite and spiritual leadership of the country.

Released in 1963, Fr Dumitru resumed his post as Professor of Dogmatics at the Theological Institute in Bucharest. When, some years later and shortly before his retirement, he was granted a limited freedom to travel and to engage with Christians outside the Soviet region in the ecumenical dialogue in which he delighted, he could never have referred openly to conditions in Romania or to the restrictions under which writers and thinkers had to work there, without incurring grave risk to himself as well as to his wife and daughter. The friends who welcomed him or who were able themselves to visit him in Romania had, on their part, to exercise considerable discretion. Of the years he spent in prison he said nothing in public and very little in private.

It is against this scantily-sketched background that the following text should be read. Depths of human experience as well as a commanding intellect and a profound Christian vision are behind it. We have it at two removes from the speaker's mother tongue, but it retains the character of the original address, as well as something of the quality of his speech and message.

Short as it is, this essay strikes several of the keynotes of the first volume of his major work, *Orthodox Dogmatic Theology,* published in 1978 and translated into English in 1994.[2] Canon Allchin recalls two occasions which illustrate the intimate relation between eternity and time expounded in this essay: 'Once in Romania, we were gazing at a panorama of the snow-covered Carpathians; and another time, in England, looking up at Durham Cathedral high above the wooded slopes of the River Wear. On both occasions Fr Dumitru said with emphasis: "*That* cannot be absent from eternity."'

---

[2] Dumitru Stăniloae, *Orthodox Dogmatic Theology: The Experience of God,* trans. Ioan Ionita and Robert Barringer, foreword by Kallistos Ware (Holy Cross Orthodox Press, 1994).

In Fr Dumitru, delight in the beauty and goodness of creation as the gift of Divine Love whose supreme expression is the Incarnation of the Word, lived unquenched alongside all that he knew of suffering and the distortion of sin. This talk, given in a dark time, mediates a vision which can refresh and fortify the faith of Christians today.

In this new edition, Fr Dumitru's talk is accompanied by an essay by Metropolitan Kallistos Ware, an edited transcript of his University Sermon, preached in the University Church of St Mary the Virgin, Oxford, on Sunday 11 June 1989 that was originally published in the Winter 1989 volume of *Fairacres Chronicle*. It is particularly apposite to bring these two essays together, since Ware provided the foreword to the English translation of *Orthodox Dogmatic Theology*, where the precepts explored in 'Eternity and Time' are greatly expanded.[3] In his foreword Ware tells us of Fr Dumitru that, 'first and fundamentally, his is a theology of *love and personal communion*. The only possible way to talk about God and humankind, he believes, is to use the language of love.'[4] While apparent in the essay published here, the same could be said of Ware's own theology.

In the essay reproduced here, informed by Fr Dumitru's writing, Ware offers his own reflections, drawing on his own experience and understanding of time in relation to God. He examines the sensations of loss or unreality that we may feel with the passing of time, but focusses on the potential for beauty in that experience as well. In his words, 'the meaning of time is to be found in relationship, in personal communion, in response and openness to others'.

THE EDITORS

---

[3] Ware's introduction includes an extended biography of Fr Dumitru.

[4] Ware, in Stăniloae, *Orthodox Dogmatic Theology,* Preface xix.

TIME

ETERNITY & TIME
DUMITRU STĂNILOAE

In Christianity there are two concepts of God, one that comes from the Bible and which belongs to Christian life and experience, and the other that comes from Greek philosophy. The first presents God as the living God, full of concern and interest for humankind. The second presents God as unmoved and immoveable. Eastern Orthodoxy has made a significant effort to combine and harmonize the two conceptions. It has sought to reconcile both these ways of thinking about God by means of the doctrine of the Divine Essence and the Divine Energies—by saying that while in His essence God remains unmoved, He comes out of himself in His energies.

This is to think of God in a personal way, for a person exists on many levels at once. A mother for instance, when playing with her child, is descending to the level of the child whilst at the same time remaining an adult; likewise God who enters into the world remains at the same time beyond and above the world. Today, Western theology is also trying to exceed the notion of God as simply unmoved, but sometimes, as for example in Tillich, it rushes to the other extreme and thinks of God as only in process, in becoming, in movement.[1] We try to reconcile the unchangeableness of God on the one hand and his living character on the other, in the spirit of St Gregory Palamas (*c.* 1296–1359), the great Byzantine theologian of the

[1] E.g. Paul Tillich, *Systematic Theology*, 3 vols. (University of Chicago Press, 1973).

fourteenth century, seeking to show the link between the eternity of God and our human life within time.

Eternity

Eternity cannot simply be an unchangeable substance, it cannot be like an eternal self-subsistent law. Such an eternity would not be inexhaustible, and the fact that it is inexhaustible arises from its interiority, which is like that of personal existence. Eternity must include an interior dimension and freedom of will. Only thus can it be inexhaustible, a source of continual newness. If we think of the eternity of God simply in terms of pure reason, or of an eternal substance, then we have a false picture of eternity not the true one. Eternity must be a fullness of life, and therefore true eternity must be the eternity of God, God being perceived as a subject who is true and always the same in himself, but who at the same time is the source of an eternal and infinite variety of manifestations.

However, true personal life only exists where there is communion, and there is no fullness of life without fullness of communion. Fullness of life therefore subsists in perfect communion between perfect subjects, perfect persons. So the true eternity is that of the Holy Trinity. The Trinity of Persons is the fullness both of communion and of eternity. The Holy Trinity remains eternally unchangeable in its love, but its love is fullness of life and therefore there is inexhaustible potential for variation in its manifestation and action.

Eternity is life and life is movement. Karl Barth has rightly said that what is purely and simply unmoving and unmoved is dead, and that if God is entirely unmoved, then to be God is to be dead![2] But the kind of movement which is always the same—

[2] Karl Barth, *Church Dogmatics*, Vol. 2.1, 'The Doctrine of God', trans. J. L. M. Haire (T&T Clark, 1957), 494.

the automatic movement of a machine—is also dead. The true meaning of eternity can be found only in the perfect communion which exists between eternal Persons whose love is inexhaustible. And anyone who shares in such a divine interpersonal communion receives into themselves eternal life. 'And this is eternal life, that they may know you, the only true God, and Jesus Christ whom you have sent.' (John 17:3) The inexhaustible life of God as Persons in communion cannot consist in simply passing from one concern or one thought to another: the eternal life of the perfect subjectivity does not depend on finite realities, rather these finite realities depend upon the eternity of God. The life of the eternal subjectivity of God must be a fullness which is not just passing away. It consists in love towards persons of an equal plenitude; thus it is an eternal, an inexhaustible life. It involves a relationship with the other who responds with a similar love. The Divine Persons love one another with an eternally inexhaustible love proper to themselves. They love one another as partners in a complete reciprocity, a mutuality of sharing. It is a continual movement which passes from one to another in the mutual exchange of the same eternal and perfect love.

Eternity understood in this way as a personal communion of life must not be thought of as irreconcilable with time. Time is not a sin against eternity, a fall from eternity, something opposed to it. The eternity of God as life in its plenitude, as an eternal and perfect love between the Persons who are perfectly in union with one another, carries within itself the possibility of time. Time, on the other hand, carries within itself the possibility of eternity which can be realized in communion with God by His grace; for God can enter into a relationship of love with temporal beings. We would underline that this actualization of eternity in time is always by God's grace, because it is God who has made us as beings capable of responding to Him in the first place, and it is He who makes us the offer of His love. Thus it is

He who has given us this link with eternity, and it is in communion with Him that we obtain eternity.

Time

Love is the gift of oneself to another, and the waiting for the full return of that gift from the other in response. Only in a complete and immediate response to the offer of love is love fully realized and full communion attained between the two. The interval of waiting for the response is time. As such, time represents a spiritual distance between persons, while eternity is beyond all distance or separation. St Maximos the Confessor (*d.* 662) says:

> The mystery of Pentecost is thus the direct union of those who are in the providence of God, with the Providence of God himself. That is to say, the union of our created nature with the Word of God by the operation of God's goodness is a union in which there is no longer time or becoming.[3]

Within the Holy Trinity the interval of waiting for the response is reduced to nothing, because the gift of one Person to the other is immediate. The Divine Love between the three Persons is thus always complete and perfect.

In creating others to be partners of His Trinitarian love, God has seen that, because they are created, they cannot respond in the same way, but only in a limited and finite way. For them, response implies freedom of will, effort and growth. Our human reply cannot be simultaneously this total gift of ourselves, as prompt and immediate as God's offer of His love to us. For this reason, God offers His love in proportion to our growth and our capacity to respond. In this way God communicates himself to us gradually so that we can learn to grow at our own pace in response to Him.

---

[3] Quoted in *The Philokalia*, trans. G. E. H. Palmer (Faber & Faber, 2011), vol. 2, 392.

This gradual and slow movement in response to God is equivalent to time. And God is always ready to help us grow towards the eternity of complete and immediate response to the love He offers us. As we journey towards eternity, God himself lives with us in time, sharing our expectation on the way, through the operation of His energies and through His relationships with us. This is so because, in offering His love, He voluntarily accepts and lives limitation; we can see this in the whole history of salvation as it is gradually realized in time. God lives His eternity fully in His own Trinitarian relationships, and at the same time He lives that same eternity in coming out to meet us in time. This is kenosis, the descent of God into time and space, willingly accepted by Him for the sake of His creation and lived simultaneously with the eternity of His Trinitarian life.

This means that it is also necessary for us to respond, not only in our life within time, but also in our relationship to eternity from which this offer comes to us. God waits with long patience for our return to Him, for us to wake up to the understanding of the love He offers. At the same time He rejoices in the complete absence of interval or hesitation in the interchange of love between the trinitarian Persons. What heightens the paradox of God's relationship with us is that the joy of the supernatural love within the Trinity is increased as God waits for the response of His human creatures—or is lessened by their slowness to return, 'Listen! I am standing at the door, knocking; if you hear my voice and open the door, I will come in to you and eat with you, and you with me.' (Rev. 3:20).

For God, time means the duration of the expectant waiting between His knocking on the door and our act of opening it to Him. Time in this sense also implies the freedom of humanity and the great respect that God has for His creatures; God does not enter our hearts by force. Union with God in love can only be realized in our free response to the offer of this love; that is why God gives us time; and because of the respect which God has for his creation, this time is lived both by God and us. To put it another way, God—in waiting for our response—lives in time without forgetting His eternity or leaving it; while we, when we do not hear His voice, live a time which is without any consciousness of eternity.

There can be no question that when we do not hear the voice of God, or choose not to respond to it, we are simply waiting; we wait for all kinds of things, and as a result we live totally immersed in time. But when what we are waiting for is an event of great personal importance to us, then we become more conscious of the passage of time. And this waiting for some great event always has something joyful in it that occupies the soul and drives away its boredom. The most intense expectation or waiting, the greatest desire of all, is for the unreserved love of another person.

Thus we live eternity in hope, in anticipation, and this fills us with joy to overflowing, so that we are no longer conscious of the passing of time. God is with us in this waiting in hope for the love of human persons. He does everything to make this response possible; He is never discouraged as we are, and never switches His attention to other, unimportant things, as we do. He never finds time boring as we do. God's vision of things extends deep into the fullness of the future and therefore He is much more patient than we are and is content when things are not complete; He does not give up hope in the way that we do.

Growing towards God

God wishes us to be always growing in our love for Him, He continually gives us, by His acts, the Divine Energies which strengthen us to grow into a fullness of response. In this sense, one can speak of God in history—as it were in 'becoming'—at the level of His actions which are directed towards us. He advances with us towards what we are to become. However, in us the process of becoming is not *just* a matter of the interval that separates us from full union with God, not just a matter of our travelling towards Him. Because we can sense a continual increase all along the way in the loving atmosphere of His presence, we can say that our time too is gradually being filled with an ever-greater awareness of eternity. God, by waiting with hope for our response, himself brings eternity into time. Nor does the interval between the offer of God and our response necessarily have to be reduced gradually. Human beings can respond rapidly—and there are some who do respond very rapidly to God—but others disappoint His expectation:

> Jerusalem, Jerusalem, the city that kills the prophets and stones those who are sent to it! How often have I desired to gather your children together as a hen gathers her brood under her wings, and you were not willing! (Matt. 23:37)

God announces the future through His prophets, and this shows that His works are to be understood in and through time, though He himself is beyond it. We are moved inwardly by God's call, even if we respond only hesitantly. God is like a great arch spanning the gap between His offer and the response of humanity, between eternity and time, and thus the person in time feels themselves to be drawing close to eternity. Only when someone has become completely oblivious to the offer of God, altogether unresponsive—when they no longer have any intention of responding to it—only then is that person altogether lost to this movement towards eternity. God makes His eternity efficacious by helping us to overcome this distance in time between ourselves and Him and between ourselves and others. The love of God which works in time is full of His love because it is in eternity, and this is what makes it so powerful. Acting within time, His love draws us beyond time.

Whenever people perceive the love of God and respond to it in some measure, they live eternity. Indeed, in a certain way, whenever they live in love between themselves, they live eternity. This understanding of time as always moving towards eternity helps us to see how it is that we are always turning towards the future, always looking further towards what we have not yet discovered and that we have never fully arrived at in this life. Time manifests the fact that we do not rest and cannot rest in what we are, but are always turned towards that state in which we shall be able to rest wholly in God. Time shows us that we are suspended over the abyss of nothingness. That is why we are always searching for a fuller understanding of what we are and of what is around us: we cannot fully understand the meaning of things in this life within time. The present moment is always a moment that is extended in expectation towards the future. It isn't *only* a present moment. 'For here we have no lasting city' (Heb. 13:14), that is to say 'a present' in the full sense of the word. Only God, the fullness of being, has that eternal present. Through time we move towards a fuller response to God, to the offer of His love, and God himself draws us on into our true existence. For this reason we need to look beyond the present moment, working in it for the future in order to find our true existence in eternity. Leaving the things which are behind we press forward towards those things which are yet to be. That which is in the present is in the process of dying.

Time is like the distance between the two ends of a bridge. There is something ambiguous, uncertain about it. It is a state of movement in the direction either of death or fullness of life. It is the flight from Egypt through the desert of Sinai towards Canaan; the flight of Lot from Sodom towards another place, passing through a country where he cannot remain. To remain stationary is to die: we must move on, renouncing this state threatened by death in the sure faith that we shall find the fullness of life.

In practice this means no longer living to ourselves but living to Him whom we shall find only by dying to ourselves. We accept the loss of an apparent life so as to find the true life; it means conquering death by death. But only when this acceptance of death to oneself means living to the supreme Person of God, only then does this death bring us to the true life. 'For those who want to save their life will lose it, and those who lose their life for my sake will find it.' (Matt. 16:25). St Cyril of Alexandria (376–444) says, 'One can only enter into the presence of God in the state of sacrifice', of voluntary death to oneself.[4]

On the other hand, the person who goes out from themselves simply in order to acquire more things, does not advance towards life but only towards death. Using time only to advance ourselves, we strengthen our own selfishness. Such a time filled with self is not really time at all because it is no longer an interval separating human persons, still less separating the human from the Divine Person. The time that we live in selfishness apart from God is only an apparent time, because we are not going out from ourselves to another person. Time which is only an interval between a person and the things they want to snatch, or between themselves and other persons considered as things to be dominated and exploited, is not properly time at all; it is simply a going forward in the desert of oneself towards total death.

Time is only real, and in this sense positive and creative, when it is understood as an interval in which persons go out to meet one another, and ultimately in which persons go out to meet the Person of God. Time is only real and creative when a person is advancing, in his journey through time, towards the union of his own life with that of others and with the infinite life of God. Time is a real movement of the human person beyond themselves, in order to reduce the distance between themselves

[4] Cyril of Alexandria, *Sermon XCIX*, commentary on Luke.

and God. Only in passing through time as a real journey do we reach eternity—not by trying to escape from time—because we pass through this real interval only insofar as we unite ourselves in love with the supreme Person of God. As long as we remain shut up in ourselves, God draws away from us, because we draw away from other people and cannot enter into personal communion with them.

Barriers to Union with God

In this life we never enter fully into this union with God because sin always holds us back. We must find the supreme Person of God through the person of our neighbour, and if we did not find God in and through them we should not truly find our neighbour either, nor would we find what is continually true and new in that, that which in God or our neighbour helps us to go out from ourselves and gives us life. In this way, going beyond time into eternity in no way takes us out of the realm of interpersonal relations as it would according to a Platonist or philosophical conception of eternity.

We can only really grow in personal communion with another if the other gives themselves freely to us, is not dominated or snatched by us, or pushed to us by others. Only between persons can there be this free and complete mutual gift of life. We go out to one another in love. But we do not have the strength to give ourselves completely to the other unless the other has already invited us to do so. This is why St Cyril of Alexandria says that we can only come before the presence of the Father in a state of sacrifice, when Christ is in us and His sacrifice is at work within us.

Because we are not willing to simplify things by making a full response of love to God, we encounter many problems and difficulties on our way. As long as we have a kind of spiritual hesitation in ourselves, time always has a double possibility: it can be a time of rising towards God or of falling towards a black eternity. Time in this sense will come to an end only when we have either made a complete and immediate response to the call of God, or when we have finally and definitively confined ourselves in our own solitude, where there is no call and no longer any possibility of response. A constant refusal to respond to the offer of love fixes the creature spiritually in the total impossibility of communication. Here there is no more waiting, no more hope, no more expectation. It is doubtful whether, in that state, it means anything to speak about time at all, still less about the fullness of eternity.

Since in this condition there is no longer anything new, all we can properly speak about is an image of eternity turned completely inside out, the extreme opposite of true eternity: time made meaningless and useless by total emptiness; the absence of all movement, of any direction or goal. The endless monotony of emptiness and the fullness of communion represent the two radically different aspects of eternity. The first is the eternity of death and the second the eternity of life.

Time that can advance towards the fullness of true eternity is itself creative. It draws from the life of the infinite energies of God, and transfuses them into the created world. Time fixed in an unchangeable monotony no longer has anything of this true character. Properly speaking it is no longer time at all, because it is no longer a succession of states in which there is always something new. It becomes an eternity of emptiness and monotony in which hope is no longer possible, 'Abandon hope all you who enter here'. This is a time that is utterly devoid of meaning and succession. It is an endless state of existence as damnation, as petrifaction, as conscious death. It is the immobility or black eternity of hell, the uttermost shadow and darkness of existence; the absence of life, lived as torture.

The unchangeable character of God, which He shares with those who grow in love, is the unchangeableness of the fullness of His life of love, beyond which there can be nothing else. The unchangeableness of hell is the total absence of life. Those in this condition have entirely broken off the dialogue which kept them within the movement of love drawing them towards eternity. Strictly speaking, their life is no longer a life, their existence no longer an existence: for them time means only becoming.

If we say that God is entirely in a process of becoming, it means that we no longer see in Him the fullness of life and therefore no longer recognize fullness of life as a possibility for His creatures. Becoming is nourished from the fullness of God. As long as there is a chance of becoming, of movement, there is a link with God.

The Bridge between Time and Eternity

God offers himself to created beings through the creatures which He has made, and through His energies; but in Christ He offers himself as hypostasis, as Person. In Christ, full communion with the person of God himself is accessible to us at our own level. Christ bridges the interval between divinity and humanity, and the interval between himself as God and ourselves. However, for us in the present, this condition is realized only in principle and virtually. The human will of Christ responds fully to this Divine Will, but that does not negate the distinction between them. The Divine Will of Christ always remains that which offers, calls, demands a response, and which makes response possible; the human will of Christ remains always that which does respond. But at the same time, the fact that the human will of Christ responds on our behalf, asks on our behalf, remains in communion with our temporal condition—with our aspirations and our griefs—means that Christ lives *as God* these links with humankind in its temporality.

As long as we cannot all fully and perfectly respond to the offer of God's love, Christ himself remains linked with us in our humanity, in our temporality, more closely than God was linked with us before the Incarnation; even though it is He who has brought into our temporal condition the dawn of eternity and the power of a more complete response on our part to the offer of God. The Incarnation of the Word of God, and the fact that in Him both His being linked with us in our temporal condition and His transcendence of any temporal interval between us and God exist together, also shows us the inward link between the eternity of God and the temporal condition of humanity. St Maximos the Confessor, in refuting the theory of the Origenists that time is the product of the Fall and that the Fall is the origin of movement, made it clear that movement, and consequently time and becoming, are all the products of God's creative act and are advancing towards Him.[5]

It is not on account of the Fall that movement and change have come about, but because it is the will of God the Trinity to draw us towards himself through movement and change. The movement of time is sustained by the fullness of God's eternity. The Son of God has become incarnate to help us to pass through and beyond this movement, this temporal interval that separates us from full communion with one another and with Him. In a mysterious way He makes this movement with us. This is the way in which Christ is with us in time although He is simultaneously beyond time.

Following the text in Hebrews 11:39–40, Origen himself has given this remarkable commentary on our Lord's words, "I tell you, I will never again drink of this fruit of the vine until that day when I drink it new with you in my Father's kingdom." (Matt. 26:29):

---

[5] Cf. Origen, *The Ambigua*, Patrologia Graeca 91, 1073B–C.

He waits that we should return, that we should follow his example, that we should go with him in order himself to rejoice with us and to drink with us the wine of the kingdom, in the kingdom of his Father. For the present, because he is merciful, he weeps with us with great compassion, with greater compassion than the Apostle himself weeping with those who weep, and rejoicing with those who rejoice. ... In drawing near to the Father and in finding himself near to the cross of sacrifice and offering his sacrifice for us, he does not drink the fruit of the vine, because coming near to the altar of sacrifice means precisely not drinking of the wine of joy, because he suffers until the fullness of time the bitterness of our sins.[6]

One sees how Christ is, at one and the same time, wholly in the complete offering of himself to the Father, that is to say in the transcendence of any temporal interval in the fullness of eternity, but at the same time truly united and bound together with us who suffer within time. It is precisely thus that He gives himself for us. Origen continues:

How long will Christ wait? He says, 'Until I have finished my work.' And when will he finish this work? When he will bring me to perfection, me who am the least and greatest of all sinners. Then he will have finished his work. Until that time he will not be fully subordinate to the Father, nor will he offer up everything to the Father. He does not offer himself to the Father for himself, but for me in whom the work is not yet finished. For this reason he says, 'It is not yet finished.'[7]

Christ's joy will not be complete until the whole of His Body also enters into joy. Since we are all members of His Body, as long as there are any of us who are not fully and completely submitted to the Father, Christ himself is not fully submitted to the Father. Neither will the Saints departed be in the fullness of

[6] Origen, *Homiliae in Leviticum,* 7.2.41–6, 51–4, ed. M. Borret, Sources Chretiennes 286 (Cerf, 1967–9), 310/312.

[7] Origen, *Homiliae in Leviticum,* 7.2.62–6, 68–72, ed. Borret, 312/314.

joy as long as they weep for our sins, which means: as long as I have not passed beyond the temporal interval that exists in time between myself and everyone else, time remains for me an objective reality. This same idea is taken up by St John Chrysostom (347–407), by St Maximos the Confessor and later by Pascal (1623–1662) who said those wonderful words, 'Jesus will be in agony until the end of the world.'[8] The eternal weeps for humanity in time. Eternity has entered into solidarity with time while remaining distinct from it. Eternity is the origin and the goal of time. This is the great consolation that Christianity gives to humankind.

[8] Blaise Pascal, *Pensées*, Section 7, Pensée 553, 'Le Mystère de Jésus', ed. M. Autrand (Bordas, 1965), 164.

TIME: PRISON OR PATH TO FREEDOM?

KALLLISTOS WARE

Be careful then how you live, not as unwise people but as wise, making the most of the time, because the days are evil.
(Eph. 5:15–16)

Circle, Line, Spiral

It is a striking fact, easily overlooked, that in the New Testament Jesus Christ begins His public ministry by speaking of time, and that He likewise refers to time in the last conversation that He has with His disciples at the very end of His earthly life. "The time is fulfilled" (Mark 1:15): so Christ commences His preaching, while immediately before His Ascension He says to the eleven: 'It is not for you to know the times or periods that the Father has set by his own authority.' (Acts 1:7). Both at the outset and at the conclusion of the story the question of time confronts us: time as fulfilled in Christ, time as a mystery still hidden in God. What, then, do we mean by time? Since the theme of time is in this way deeply embedded in the Gospel narrative, we cannot dismiss the question as no more than a speculative issue, of interest merely to the professional philosopher. It is a matter that concerns each one of us personally. Philip Larkin's query is posed to us all:

> What are days for? Days are where we live.
> They come, they wake us Time and time over…
> Where can we live but days?[1]

[1] Philip Larkin, *Collected Poems* (Marvell Press, 1988), 67.

'What are days for?' The question is not simply 'What is time?' but 'What is time *for*?' We are concerned not just with the abstract essence of time but with its practical effect on our lives. What are we to do about time, what are we to make of it?

Oscar Cullmann, in his classic work *Christ and Time*, offers two basic images of time.[2] It may be seen as cyclical, as a circle, ring or wheel; or else it may be seen as linear, as a straight path, a river or an arrow. Without asserting too sharp a dichotomy between Hellenism and Judaism, it may be said that the first manner of envisaging time is characteristically Greek—in Aristotle's words, 'For indeed time itself seems to be a sort of circle'[3]—while the second approach predominates in Hebraic and Iranian thought. Not that the two symbols need be mutually exclusive, for they both embody an aspect of the truth. The image of the circle reflects the recurrent rhythms in the world of nature, the line expresses our sense of time as direction, progress and evolution.

What strikes us at once is that these symbols are both double-edged. The circle of time may be felt as redemptive, as the means of our return to the golden age, to the lost paradise; or it may be viewed as meaningless repetition, as boredom and futility. It may serve as an image of celestial eternity—Henry Vaughan's 'great ring of pure and endless light'[4]—or it may be a sign of hell, a closed and vicious circle. So it is with linear time. It is true that the line may be strictly horizontal, and therefore neutral. But equally it may be seen as oblique or sloping, and in that case inclined either upward or downward. Interpreted positively, the line of time becomes a path of ascent to the summit

---

[2] Oscar Cullmann, *Christ and Time: The Primitive Christian Conception of Time and History* (Wipf & Stock, 3rd edn. 2018).

[3] Aristotle, *Physics* iv, 14 (223b29).

[4] Henry Vaughan, 'The World', in *A Great Ring of Pure and Endless Light: Selected Poems* (Crescent Moon Publishing, 2012).

of the holy mountain; understood negatively, it signifies deterioration and decline, 'downhill all the way': *Facilis descensus Averni...* Once more the image is equivocal.

A better symbol of time than either the circle or the line is surely the spiral, combining elements from both of the other figures, yet avoiding their more blatant defects. The spiral, more truly than the circle or the line, reflects the basic patterns in the physical universe, from the movement of the galaxies to the folds in the human cerebral cortex. It includes the cyclic rhythms of nature, yet in the case of the spiral the circle is not closed but suggests continuous advance towards a goal. Above all, the spiral has the advantage of being—at any rate in some instances—three-dimensional, thus expressing our post-Einsteinian sense of living in a space-time continuum. St Dionysius the Areopagite (5th–6th century AD) regarded the spiral as the highest type of movement, the form most befitting the angelic powers,[5] and that strange prophetic figure of twelfth-century Italy, Joachim of Fiore (1135–1202), thought the same; I am inclined to agree with them. Once more, however, the question confronts us: what kind of spiral? For spirals can be either descending or ascending, or rather they may be both these things at once, as the sailor discovered in Poe's short story, *A Descent into the Maelström*.[6] What, then, is to be our perception of time's spiral: a descending vortex, sucking us down into annihilation, or the never-ending dance of love, drawing us 'farther up and farther in'?[7]

---

[5] Dionysius the Areopagite, *The Divine Names*, iv, 8. On the symbolism of the spiral, see Jill Purce, *The Mystic Spiral: Journey of the Soul* (Thames and Hudson, 1974).

[6] Edgar Allan Poe, 'A Descent into the Maelström', first publ. in *Graham's Magazine* XVIII/5 (May 1841), 235–241.

[7] C. S. Lewis, *The Last Battle* (Penguin, 1956, repr. 1975), 158 and passim.

Enemy or Friend?

Our experience of time, as these three symbols indicate, is deeply ambivalent. How are we to regard time: as enemy or friend, as our prison or our path to freedom? Which aspect do we find predominant in its double-edged impact upon us: anguish or healing, terror or hope, decay or growth, separation or relationship? If the second edition of *The Oxford Dictionary of Quotations* can be trusted as a guide, time has commonly been seen more as a threat than as an enrichment. We find Shakespeare castigating 'envious and calumniating time';[8] in Ben Jonson's eyes time is 'that old bald cheater';[9] 'Time with a gift of tears', writes Swinburne,[10] while Tennyson calls time 'a maniac scattering dust'.[11] Others, it is true, refer to time in more constructive terms as a gardener or a physician, but they are minority voices. For Isaac Watts, time with its irreversible flow brings about a sense of loss and unreality:

> Time, like an ever-rolling stream,
> Bears all its sons away:
> They fly forgotten, as a dream
> Dies at the opening day.[12]

An equally sombre view is to be found in the main Biblical work devoted to the theme of time, Ecclesiastes. In the opening chapter the Preacher sees time as vain repetition, as the cause of 'weariness' and disillusion:

---

[8] *Troilus and Cressida*, Act III, scene iii.

[9] *The Poetaster*, Act I, scene i.

[10] 'The Garden of Proserpine', in *Poems and Ballads by Algernon Charles Swinburne* (J. Cadmen Hotten, 1873), 196, v.3.

[11] 'In Memoriam', section L, in *The Complete Poetical Works of Tennyson* (The Riverside Press, 1898), 162.

[12] 'Our God, Our Help', in *The Psalms and Hymns of Isaac Watts* (Soli Deo Gloria, 1997), 157.

All is vanity…
One generation passes away,
        and another generation comes…
The wind blows to the south,
        and goes round to the north;
round and round goes the wind,
        and on its circuits the wind returns.
All streams run to the sea,
        but the sea is not full;
to the place where the streams flow,
        there they flow again.
All things are full of weariness…
        and there is nothing new under the sun.   (Eccl. 1:2–9)

Taken as a whole, however, the Scriptural attitude towards time is markedly less hostile than this. The Preacher, in a later section, links time with beauty and with eternity:

> For everything there is a season, and a time for every matter under heaven … He has made everything suitable for its time; moreover, he has put a sense of past and future into their minds.' (Eccl. 3:1, 11).

In the New Testament this positive approach is reaffirmed. 'The time is fulfilled' (Mark 1:15): time is not pointless but purposive; Christ comes in the fullness of time. So, far from being meaningless and arbitrary, time is something which 'the Father has set by his own authority' (Acts 1:7). St Paul speaks of 'an acceptable time' or 'a day of salvation' (2 Cor. 6:2); time can be 'redeemed' (Eph. 5:16). God has made the 'ages' or 'aeons' of time (cf. Heb. 1:2), and He is 'the King of the ages' (1 Tim. 1:17). There is no doubt about the biblical view: time is part of God's creation, and as such it is 'all together good and beautiful' (Gen. 1:31 [LXX]).

Bisecting the World of Time

If we are to appreciate the beauty of time at its full value,· then there are two basic truths that need to be kept in view. First, time and eternity are not opposed but interdependent, not mutually exclusive but complementary. Second, the meaning of time is to be found, as Stăniloae says, in relationship, in personal communion, in response and openness to others.[13] Time is not to be interpreted merely in privative terms as a reflection of human finitude and a restriction to our liberty, but it is a positive expression of what it signifies to be a person, an indispensable precondition of human freedom and love. In relation to both of these truths, the key to the right understanding of time is provided by Christ's Incarnation.

Time and eternity are not opposed. When Spinoza maintains, 'Eternity cannot be defined by time or have any relation to it',[14] the second part of this statement, at any rate, is definitely open to question. Indeed, the Incarnation involves precisely an 'intersection of the timeless with time', to use T. S. Eliot's phrase in the *Four Quartets*.[15] As he puts it in 'The Rock', Christ's birth is an event within time and yet transforming time:

---

[13] See above, pp. 10–11. Stăniloae's talk as printed in this book was considerably expanded to form the first part of volume 1 of his *Teologia dogmatica ortodoxa* (3 vols., Bucharest, 1978). Quotations are taken either from the essay above or from the longer version in the English translation, *Orthodox Dogmatic Theology: The Experience of God*, 3 vols. trans. Ioan Ionita and Robert Barringer (Holy Cross Orthodox Press, 1994), vol. 1, 172–213.

[14] Spinoza, *Ethics*, Part V, proposition xxiii, note: trans. A. Boyle (Everyman's Library, 1910), 214; quoted in Maurice Nicoll, *Living Time and the Integration of Life* (Shambhala, 1984), 132.

[15] T. S. Eliot, *Four Quartets*, 'The Dry Salvages', *The Complete Poems and Plays* (Faber and Faber, 1969), 189–90.

> Then came, at a predetermined moment, a moment in time and of time,
> A moment not out of time, but in time, in what we call history: transecting, bisecting the world of time, a moment in time but not like a moment of time,
> A moment in time but time was made through that moment: for without the meaning there is no time, and that moment of time gave the meaning.[16]

'Transecting, bisecting the world of time': Eliot's point is brought out vividly in the *Protevangelion* or *Book of James*, when Joseph speaks of time as standing still at the moment of the Nativity:

> Now I Joseph was walking, and I walked not. And I looked up into the air and saw the air in amazement. And I looked up to the pole of heaven and saw it standing still, and the birds of the heaven without motion. And I looked upon the earth and saw a dish set, and workmen reclining beside it, and their hands were in the dish: and they that were chewing did not chew, and they that were lifting the food did not lift it, and they that were putting it into their mouth did not put it in, but the faces of them all were looking upward. And behold there were sheep being driven, and they did not move forward but stood still; and the shepherd lifted his hand to strike them with his staff, and his hand remained in the air. And I looked at the stream of the river and saw the mouths of the kids upon the water, and they did not drink. Then suddenly all things moved onward on their course.[17]

What can be affirmed to a supreme degree concerning the time of the Incarnation is likewise true, at least potentially, of every moment of time. At the Incarnation eternity transects time in a unique manner. Yet each moment of time is also open to

---

[16] T. S. Eliot, *Complete Poems and Plays*, 160.

[17] *Protevangelion* xviii, 2: ed. C. Tischendorf, *Evangelia Apocrypha* (Hermann Mendelssohn, 1876), 34–5; trans. M. R. James, *The Apocryphal New Testament* (Clarendon Press, 1924), 46 (translation adapted).

eternity; at each moment it is possible for eternity to break into the temporal sequence, assuming time into itself and so transforming it. Eternity is not simply outside the moments of time but rather is at the heart of each moment; and this eternity, present within time, gives to time its true value. 'Eternity is as much in time as it is above time', writes Fr Stăniloae.[18]

Plato was not far from the truth when he spoke of time as a moving image of eternity.[19] Time and eternity—and, by the same token, space and infinity—do not contradict but complete one another. Time and space, while modalities of the created order, are rooted in God's eternal, uncreated life and find their fulfilment there. Between time and eternity there exists, to use the phrase of the French Orthodox author Olivier Clément (1921–2009), 'a marriage bond', *un rapport proprement nuptial*.[20] In the words of St Maximos the Confessor, 'The inner principles [*logoi*, 'reasons'] of time abide in God.'[21] The Divine Eternity, writes Fr Stăniloae, 'carries within itself the possibility of time. Time, on the other hand, carries within itself the possibility of eternity'.[22] Eternity is turned towards time and goes out to meet it; and time, when taken up into eternity, is not annihilated but transfigured.

Time as Freedom to Love

Time, from a Christian perspective, is one of the means whereby God evokes and guarantees our created human freedom, our freedom to love. The notion of freedom—both Divine Freedom

---

[18] Stăniloae, *Orthodox Dogmatic Theology*, vol. 1, 158.

[19] Cf. Plato, *Timaeus* 37d.

[20] Olivier Clément, *Transfigurer le temps. Notes sur le temps à la lumière de la tradition orthodoxe* (Delachaux and Niestlé, 1959), 54.

[21] Maximos the Confessor, *Ambigua*, Patrologia Graeca 91 (Migne, 1857), 1164B.

[22] See above, p. 3.

and human freedom—is fundamental to the Christian doctrine of creation. 'God is truly present and operative only in freedom', claims Berdyaev. 'Freedom alone should be recognized as possessing a sacred quality.'[23] As Kierkegaard has rightly insisted, 'The most tremendous thing granted to humans is choice, freedom.'[24] God created the world in freedom, and He willed that the beings whom He formed in His image should likewise be free. As a Trinitarian God, a God of shared interpersonal love, He desired that we humans in our turn should be joined to Him in a relationship of mutual love. Mutual love, however, presupposes freedom, for where there is no voluntary choice there can be no love. Love cannot be constrained, but can only be tendered willingly; God is able to do anything except *compel* us to love Him. Love comes always as an offer to which the beloved is invited to respond in freedom.

By creating in this way a world of persons capable of freely responding to Him in love, God accepted to restrict, in some measure, the exercise of His omnipotence. He 'withdrew' as it were from His creation, 'distancing' himself so that His creatures might have room to love. Creation involves a divine self-limitation, what the sixteenth-century Jewish Kabbalist, Isaac Luria (1534–1572), termed *zimsum*, 'contraction' or 'concentration'.[25] In thus bringing into existence free persons with the power of rejecting Him, God inevitably took a risk. But had He not taken a risk, there would have been a universe without love. As Vladimir Lossky observes,

---

[23] Nicolas Berdyaev, *Dream and Reality: An Essay in Autobiography*, trans. Katherine Lampert (Geoffrey Bles, 1950), 46.

[24] Søren Kierkegaard, *The Journals of Søren Kierkegaard: A Selection*, trans. Alexander Dru (Oxford University Press, 1938), 372 (translation adapted).

[25] See Jürgen Moltmann, *The Trinity and the Kingdom of God* (SCM Press, 1981), 108–11.

> This divine risk, inherent in the decision to create beings in the image and likeness of God, is the summit of almighty power, or rather a surpassing of that summit in voluntarily undertaken powerlessness … He who takes no risks does not love.[26]

This risk-taking or *kenosis* on God's part, inaugurated at the creation, came to its full expression at the Incarnation. In choosing to become a creature, the Divine Creator embraced a situation of complete vulnerability, an entire and unreserved solidarity with us humans in our pain and brokenness. He willed to effect our salvation, not through any exercise of transcendent power, but through the utter powerlessness of His incarnate state 'for power is made perfect in weakness.' (2 Cor. 12:9). Such exactly is the supreme paradox of Christology: God is never so strong as when He is most weak, never so truly divine as when He empties himself. St Gregory of Nyssa (*d.* 395) saw this clearly:

> The fact that the omnipotent nature should have been capable of descending to the humiliated condition of humanity provides a clearer proof of power than great and supernatural miracles… His descent to our lowliness is the supreme expression of His power.[27]

Nestorius (386–451) made the same point: 'All greatness grows great by self-abasement, and not by exalting itself.'[28] The reason why God chose to save us not by force but with our voluntary consent is specifically that He loves us and therefore desires us to be free.

It is in this context of freedom and love that the meaning of time can best be appreciated. Time is part of the 'distancing'

---

[26] Vladimir Lossky, *In the Image and Likeness of God* (St Vladimir's Seminary Press, 1974), 214.

[27] Gregory of Nyssa, *Catechetical Oration* 24.

[28] Nestorius, *The Bazaar of Heracleides,* trans. G. R. Driver and L. Hodgson (Clarendon Press, 1925), 69 (translation adapted).

or 'contraction' on God's side which makes it possible for us to love freely. It is, as it were, the interspace which enables us to move towards God unconstrained and by our voluntary choice. "Listen! I am standing at the door, knocking", says Christ; "if you hear my voice and open the door, I will come in to you and eat with you, and you with me." (Rev. 3:20). God knocks, but does not break down the door; He waits for us to open it. This *waiting* on God's part is exactly the essence of time: in Fr Stăniloae's words, 'For God, time means the duration of the expectant waiting between His knocking on the door and our act of opening it to him.'[29] God issues His appeal to human freedom: *whom shall I send, and who will go for us?* After that He awaits the voluntary response from our side: 'And I said, "Here am I; send me!"' (Is. 6:8).

Time is the interval between God's appeal and our answer. We humans need this interval of time so that we may freely love God and one another; without the interval we cannot engage in the dialogue of love. On the level of uncreated divine freedom, the mutual love of the Trinity is an expression of the *totum simul*, of eternal simultaneity, and so it is without any interval of time. But on the level of created human freedom love has to be learned; and learning takes time, as we are only too well aware. Blake has well described our human condition in his *Songs of Innocence*:

> And we are put on earth a little space,
> That we may learn to bear the beams of love.[30]

Time is thus an all-important dimension of our created personhood, the setting that makes it possible for us to choose love. It is time that allows us to respond to God by our own free consent, that enables our love to mature, that permits us to grow in

---

[29] See above, page 5.

[30] *Poetry and Prose of William Blake*, ed. G. Keynes (The Nonesuch Press, 1948), 54.

love. Space is to be understood in similar terms, as an expression of God's self-distancing so that we may be free to respond to Him in love. It affords us, says Fr Stăniloae, the possibility of 'free movement … the freedom to draw near or to move away'.[31] Without time and space we cannot experience the 'between' that unites in love the 'I' and the 'Thou'. If in our daily life we commonly apprehend time very differently—not as relationship but as separation, not as freedom but as fetters upon our liberty—then that is because we are part of a fallen world in which time has become linked with mortality and death. Yet, although fallen, time is not totally so; even in our present condition we still glimpse its primal significance as a 'time of gifts' and a continual miracle. And, because it is God's creation and as such is 'all together good and beautiful', time is not to be repudiated or ignored, but redeemed. Our goal is not timelessness but time transfigured. It is true that in the Apocalypse the angel proclaims, "There shall be time no longer" (Rev. 10:6)—some would render it 'There shall be no more delay'—but the time that is to be abolished is the fallen time of death (cf. Rev. 21:4). For the Apocalypse also states that within the heavenly Jerusalem there will be 'the tree of life with its twelve kinds of fruit, producing its fruit *each month'* (Rev. 22:2, my emphasis). This can only mean that, in the eternal Kingdom of the age to come, the rhythms of cyclic time are not abolished but transformed.[32]

If the significance of time is to be found in relationship and love, it follows that true time is not simply that which is assessed mechanically by the clock or the calendar. True time is living, personal, existential, measured not by mere succession but by intention. True time is *kairos* rather than *chronos*, characterized not by the predetermined swing of the pendulum but by unpredictable yet decisive moments of opportunity, moments of

[31] Stăniloae, *Orthodox Dogmatic Theology*, vol. 1, 172.

[32] Cf. Clément, *Transfigurer le temps*, 72.

disclosure filled with meaning when clock time stands still, as Joseph found in the *Protevangelion,* and when eternity breaks in. Time is not just a fixed, unvarying pattern imposed upon us from outside, but it can be recreated from within and used as an expression of our inner selves. We are in time, but time is also in us. We speak of 'wasting time' and 'killing time', but let us also give full value to the habitual phrases 'make time', 'give time' and 'save time'.

Without the Meaning there is no Time

In my reflections on time a transition has taken place. Seeking to answer the question 'What is time?', I have been led to examine not just time itself but personhood, freedom and love. If time is discussed in the abstract and treated as a 'thing' that exists by itself, it proves ever more baffling and more elusive. St Augustine voices a difficulty familiar to us all: 'What is time? If no one asks me, I know; if I try to explain to an inquirer, I do not know.'[33] We can only begin to understand the nature of time when we take into account a whole series of other matters as well, such as our experiences of growth and decay, of being in relation, of learning to respond. 'Without the meaning there is no time':[34] and there is no such thing as absolute time, for all time is related to persons and their inner experience. Time becomes intelligible only when set in the total context of life (and death)—indeed, the two terms 'time' and 'life' are in many respects virtually interchangeable.

It is the Incarnation, we have found, that provides us with a clue to the meaning of time. As 'the moment in and out of time', to use Eliot's words,[35] it shows us the interdependence of

---

[33] Augustine of Hippo, *Confessions,* XI, 14.

[34] T. S. Eliot, 'The Rock', *Complete Poems and Plays,* 160.

[35] T. S. Eliot, 'The Dry Salvages', *Complete Poems and Plays,* 190.

time and eternity; only *sub specie aeternitatis* does time acquire its authentic resonance and depth. The Incarnation, as an act of love addressed to our human freedom, also indicates how time is to be understood in terms of personal relationship, of reciprocity and dialogue. Time, whether we choose to picture it as circle, line or spiral, is not a jailer, but the safeguard of our human personhood, the protector of liberty and love.

There are two moments in the Divine Liturgy which sum up these two aspects of time: the first is when the celebrant, immediately prior to the opening blessing, uses the words of the angels at the Incarnation, 'Glory to God in the highest heaven, and on earth peace ...' (Luke 2:14); and then the deacon says, 'It is time for the Lord to act' (Ps. 119:126). It is the vocation of time to be open to eternity; time is fulfilled when God's eternity, God's action, breaks into the temporal sequence, as happened supremely at Christ's birth in Bethlehem, as happens also at every Eucharist. The second moment comes just before the Creed, when the deacon says to the people, 'Let us love one another...', and the people reply, affirming their faith in the Father, Son and Holy Spirit. Such exactly is the true rationale of time: mutual love after the image of the Trinity.

Bibliography

Aristotle, *Physics*, Greek text with trans. by P. H. Wicksteed, F. M. Cornford, Loeb Classical Library, 228, 255 (Harvard University Press, 1934–57).

Augustine of Hippo, *Confessions*, trans. J. K. Ryan (Crown Publishing, 1960).

Karl Barth, *Church Dogmatics*, trans. J. L. M. Haire (T&T Clark, 1957).

Nicolas Berdyaev, *Dream and Reality: An Essay in Autobiography*, trans. Katherine Lampert (Geoffrey Bles, 1950).

William Blake, *Poetry and Prose*, ed. G. Keynes (The Nonesuch Press, 1948).

Olivier Clément, *Transfigurer le temps. Notes sur le temps à la lumière de la tradition orthodoxe* (Delachaux and Niestlé, 1959).

Oscar Cullmann, *Christ and Time: The Primitive Christian Conception of Time and History* (Wipf & Stock, 3rd edn. 2018).

Cyril of Alexandria, *A Commentary upon the Gospel According to S. Luke*, trans. Robert Payne Smith (Oxford University Press, 1859).

Dionysius the Areopagite, *The Divine Names*, Patrologia Graeca 3, 704C (Migne, 1857).

T. S. Eliot, *The Complete Poems and Plays* (Faber and Faber, 1969).

Gregory of Nyssa, *Oratio Catechetica*, Greek text with trans. by James Herbert Srawley (Cambridge University Press, 1903).

Søren Kierkegaard, *The Journals of Søren Kierkegaard: A Selection*, trans. Alexander Dru (Oxford University Press, 1938).

Philip Larkin, *Collected Poems*, ed. Anthony Thwaite (Marvell Press, 1988).

C. S. Lewis, *The Last Battle* (Penguin, 1956, repr. 1975).

Vladimir Lossky, *In the Image and Likeness of God* (St Vladimir's Seminary Press, 1974).

Maximos the Confessor, *Ambigua*, Patrologia Graeca 91 (Migne, 1857).

Jürgen Moltmann, *The Trinity and the Kingdom of God* (SCM Press, 1981).

Nestorius, *The Bazaar of Heracleides*, trans. G. R. Driver and L. Hodgson (Clarendon Press, 1925).

Maurice Nicoll, *Living Time and the Integration of Life* (Shambhala, 1984).

Origen, *The Ambigua*, Patrologia Graeca 91 (Migne, 1857).

Origen, *Homiliae in Leviticum*, ed. M. Borret, Sources Chretiennes 286 (Cerf, 1967–9).

Blaise Pascal, *Pensées*, ed. M. Autrand (Bordas, 1965).

The Philokalia, trans. G. E. H. Palmer (Faber & Faber, 2011).

Plato, *Timaeus*, trans. Benjamin Jowett, 5 vols. (Oxford: Clarendon Press, 1892).

Edgar Allan Poe, 'A Descent into the Maelström', *Graham's Magazine* XVIII/5 (May 1841), 235–241.

Protevangelion xviii, 2: ed. C. Tischendorf, *Evangelia Apocrypha* (Hermann Mendelssohn, 1876); trans. M. R. James, *The Apocryphal New Testament* (Clarendon Press, 1924).

Jill Purce, *The Mystic Spiral: Journey of the Soul* (Thames and Hudson, 1974).

Spinoza, *Ethics*, trans. A. Boyle (Everyman's Library, 1910).

Dumitru Stăniloae, *Orthodox Dogmatic Theology: The Experience of God*, trans. Ioan Ionita and Robert Barringer; foreword by Kallistos Ware (Holy Cross Orthodox Press, 1994).

Algernon Charles Swinburne, *Poems and Ballads* (J. Cadmen Hotten, 1873).

Tennyson, *The Complete Poetical Works*, ed. James Rolfe (The Riverside Press, 1898).

Paul Tillich, *Systematic Theology*, 3 vols. (University of Chicago Press, 1973).

Henry Vaughan, *A Great Ring of Pure and Endless Light: Selected Poems*, ed. A. H. Ninham (Crescent Moon Publishing, 2012).

Isaac Watts, *The Psalms and Hymns* (Soli Deo Gloria, 1997).

Books by Dumitru Stăniloae and Kallisto Ware published by SLG Press

Dumitru Stăniloae, *The Victory of the Cross,*
Fairacres Publications 16
(SLG Press, 1970, 3rd edn 2023)

Dumitru Stăniloae, *Prayer & Holiness: The Icon of Man Renewed in God,*
Fairacres Publications 82
(SLG Press, 1982, rev. 2023)

Kallistos Ware, *The Power of the Name: The Jesus Prayer in Orthodox Spirituality,*
Fairacres Publications 43
(SLG Press, 1974)

SLG PRESS PUBLICATIONS

FP1 *Prayer and the Life of Reconciliation* Gilbert Shaw (1969)
FP2 *Aloneness Not Loneliness* Mother Mary Clare SLG (1969)
FP4 *Intercession* Mother Mary Clare SLG (1969)
FP8 *Prayer: Extracts from the Teaching of Fr Gilbert Shaw* Gilbert Shaw (1973)
FP12 *Learning to Pray* Mother Mary Clare SLG (1970)
FP15 *Death, the Gateway to Life* Gilbert Shaw (1971)
FP16 *The Victory of the Cross* Dumitru Stăniloae (1970, 3rd edn 2023)
FP26 *The Message of Saint Seraphim* Irina Gorainov (1974)
FP28 *Julian of Norwich: Four Studies to Commemorate the Sixth Centenary of the Revelations of Divine Love* Sister Benedicta Ward SLG, Sister Eileen Mary SLG ed. A. M. Allchin (1973)
FP43 *The Power of the Name: The Jesus Prayer in Orthodox Spirituality* Kallistos Ware (1974)
FP46 *Prayer and Contemplation* and *Distractions are for Healing* Robert Llewelyn (1975)
FP48 *The Wisdom of the Desert Fathers* trans. Sister Benedicta Ward SLG (1975)
FP50 *Letters of Saint Antony the Great* trans. Derwas Chitty (1975, 2nd edn 2021)
FP54 *From Loneliness to Solitude* Roland Walls (1976)
FP55 *Theology and Spirituality* Andrew Louth (1976, rev. 1978)
FP61 *Kabir: The Way of Love and Paradox* Sister Rosemary SLG (1977)
FP62 *Anselm of Canterbury: A Monastic Scholar* Sister Benedicta Ward SLG (1973)
FP63 *Evelyn Underhill, Anglican Mystic: Two Centenary Essays* A. M. Allchin, Bishop Michael Ramsey (1977, 2nd edn 1996)
FP67 *Mary and the Mystery of the Incarnation: An Essay on the Mother of God in the Theology of Karl Barth* Andrew Louth (1977)
FP68 *Trinity and Incarnation in Anglican Tradition* A. M. Allchin (1977)
FP70 *Facing Depression* Gonville ffrench-Beytagh (1978, 2nd edn 2020)
FP71 *The Single Person* Philip Welsh (1979)
FP72 *The Letters of Ammonas, Successor of St Antony* trans. Derwas Chitty, introd. Sebastian Brock (1979, 2nd edn 2023)
FP74 *George Herbert, Priest and Poet* Kenneth Mason (1980)
FP75 *A Study of Wisdom: Three Tracts by the Author of* The Cloud of Unknowing trans. Clifton Wolters (1980)
FP78 *Silence in Prayer and Action* Sister Edmée SLG (1981)
FP81 *The Psalms: Prayer Book of the Bible* Dietrich Bonhoeffer, trans. Sister Isabel SLG (1982)
FP82 *Prayer & Holiness: The Icon of Man Renewed in God* Dumitru Stăniloae (1982, rev. 2023)
FP85 *Walter Hilton: Eight Chapters on Perfection & Angels' Song* trans. Rosemary Dorward (1983)
FP88 *Creative Suffering* Iulia de Beausobre (1989)
FP90 *Bringing Forth Christ: Five Feasts of the Child Jesus by St Bonaventure* trans. Eric Doyle OFM (1984)
FP92 *Gentleness in John of the Cross* Thomas Kane (1985)
FP93 *Prayer: The Work of the Spirit* Sister Edmée SLG (1985)
FP94 *Saint Gregory Nazianzen: Selected Poems* trans. John McGuckin (1986)
FP95 *The World of the Desert Fathers: Stories & Sayings from the Anonymous Series of the Apophthegmata Patrum* trans. Columba Stewart OSB (1986, 2nd edn 2020)

FP104 *Growing Old with God* — Timothy N. Rudd (1988, 2nd edn 2020)

FP105 *The Simplicity of Prayer: Extracts from the Teaching of Mother Mary Clare* SLG — Mother Mary Clare SLG (1988)

FP106 *Julian Reconsidered* — Kenneth Leech, Sister Benedicta Ward SLG (1988)

FP108 *The Unicorn: Meditations on the Love of God* — Harry Galbraith Miller (1989)

FP109 *The Creativity of Diminishment* — Sister Anke (1990)

FP111 *A Kind of Watershed: An Anglican Lay View of Sacramental Confession* — Christine North (1990, 2nd edn 2022)

FP116 *Jesus, the Living Lord* — Bishop Michael Ramsey (1992)

FP117 *The Spirituality of Saint Cuthbert* — Sister Benedicta Ward SLG (1992)

FP120 *The Monastic Letters of Saint Athanasius the Great* — trans. and introd. Leslie Barnard (1994, 2nd edn 2023)

FP122 *The Hidden Joy* — Sister Jane SLG, ed. Dorothy Sutherland (1994)

FP124 *Prayer of the Heart: An Approach to Silent Prayer and Prayer in the Night* — Alexander Ryrie (1995, 3rd edn 2020)

FP125 *Whole Christ: The Spirituality of Ministry* — Philip Seddon (1996)

FP127 *Apostolate and the Mirrors of Paradox* — Sydney Evans, ed. Andrew Linzey & Brian Horne (1996)

FP128 *The Wisdom of Saint Isaac the Syrian* — Sebastian Brock (1997)

FP129 *Saint Thérèse of Lisieux: Her Relevance for Today* — Sister Eileen Mary SLG (1997)

FP130 *Expectations: Five Addresses for Those Beginning Ministry* — Sister Edmée SLG (1997)

FP131 *Scenes from Animal Life: Fables for the Enneagram Types* — Waltraud Kirschke, trans. Sister Isabel SLG (1998)

FP132 *Praying the Word of God: The Use of* Lectio Divina — Charles Dumont OCSO (1999)

FP134 *The Hidden Way of Love: Jean-Pierre de Caussade's Spirituality of Abandonment* — Barry Conaway (1999)

FP135 *Shepherd and Servant: The Spiritual Theology of Saint Dunstan* — Douglas Dales (2000)

FP137 *Pilgrimage of the Heart* — Sister Benedicta Ward SLG (2001)

FP138 *Mixed Life* — Walter Hilton, trans. Rosemary Dorward (2001)

FP139 *In the Footsteps of the Lord: The Teaching of Abba Isaiah of Scetis* — John Chryssavgis & Luke Penkett (2001, 2nd edn 2023)

FP140 *A Great Joy: Reflections on the Meaning of Christmas* — Kenneth Mason (2001)

FP141 *Bede and the Psalter* — Sister Benedicta Ward SLG (2002)

FP142 *Abhishiktananda: A Memoir of Dom Henri Le Saux* — Murray Rogers, David Barton (2003)

FP143 *Friendship in God: The Encounter of Evelyn Underhill & Sorella Maria of Campello* — A. M. Allchin (2003)

FP144 *Christian Imagination in Poetry and Polity: Some Anglican Voices from Temple to Herbert* — Bishop Rowan Williams (2004)

FP145 *The Reflections of Abba Zosimas: Monk of the Palestinian Desert* — trans. and introd. John Chryssavgis (2005, 3rd edn 2022)

FP146 *The Gift of Theology: The Trinitarian Vision of Ann Griffiths and Elizabeth of Dijon* — A. M. Allchin (2005)

FP147 *Sacrifice and Spirit* — Bishop Michael Ramsey (2005)

FP148 *Saint John Cassian on Prayer* — trans. A. M Casiday (2006)

FP149 *Hymns of Saint Ephrem the Syrian* — trans. Mary Hansbury (2006)

FP150 *Suffering: Why All this Suffering? What Do I Do about It?* — Reinhard Körner OCD, trans. Sister Avis Mary SLG (2006)

FP151 *A True Easter: The Synod of Whitby 664* AD — Sister Benedicta Ward SLG (2007)

FP152 *Prayer as Self-Offering* Alexander Ryrie (2007)
FP153 *From Perfection to the Elixir: How George Herbert Fashioned a Famous Poem* Benedick de la Mare (2008)
FP154 *The Jesus Prayer: Gospel Soundings* Sister Pauline Margaret CHN (2008)
FP155 *Loving God Whatever: Through the Year with Sister Jane* Sister Jane SLG (2006)
FP156 *Prayer and Meditation for a Sleepless Night* SISTERS OF THE LOVE OF GOD (1993, 2nd edn 2009)
FP157 *Being There: Caring for the Bereaved* John Porter (2009)
FP158 *Learn to Be at Peace: The Practice of Stillness* Andrew Norman (2010)
FP159 *From Holy Week to Easter* George Pattison (2010)
FP160 *Strength in Weakness: The Scandal of the Cross* John W. Rogerson (2010)
FP161 *Augustine Baker: Frontiers of the Spirit* Victor de Waal (2010)
FP162 *Out of the Depths* Gonville ffrench-Beytagh; epilogue Wendy Robinson (1990, 2nd edn 2010)
FP163 *God and Darkness: A Carmelite Perspective* Gemma Hinricher OCD, trans. Sister Avis Mary SLG (2010)
FP164 *The Gift of Joy* Curtis Almquist SSJE (2011)
FP165 *'I Have Called You Friends': Suggestions for the Spiritual Life Based on the Farewell Discourses of Jesus* Reinhard Körner OCD (2012)
FP166 *Leisure* Mother Mary Clare SLG (2012)
FP167 *Carmelite Ascent: An Introduction to Saint Teresa and Saint John of the Cross* Mother Mary Clare SLG (rev. 2012)
FP168 *Ann Griffiths and Her Writings* Llewellyn Cumings (2012)
FP169 *The Our Father* Sister Benedicta Ward SLG (2012)
FP170 *Exploring Silence* Wendy Robinson (1974, 3rd edn 2013)
FP171 *The Spiritual Wisdom of the Syriac Book of Steps* Robert A. Kitchen (2013)
FP172 *The Prayer of Silence* Alexander Ryrie (2012)
FP173 *On Tour in Byzantium: Excerpts from The Spiritual Meadow of John Moschus* Ralph Martin SSM (2013)
FP174 *Monastic Life* Bonnie Thurston (2016)
FP175 *Shall All Be Well? Reflections for Holy Week* Graham Ward (2015)
FP176 *Solitude and Communion: Papers on the Hermit Life* ed. A. M. Allchin (2015)
FP177 *The Prayers of Jacob of Serugh* ed. Mary Hansbury (2015)
FP178 *The Monastic Hours of Prayer* Sister Benedicta Ward SLG (2016)
FP179 *The Desert of the Heart: Daily Readings with the Desert Fathers* trans. Sister Benedicta Ward SLG (2016)
FP180 *In Company with Christ: Lent, Palm Sunday, Good Friday & Easter to Pentecost* Sister Benedicta Ward SLG (2016)
FP181 *Lazarus: Come Out! Reflections on John 11* Bonnie Thurston (2017)
FP182 *Unknowing & Astonishment: Meditations on Faith for the Long Haul* Christopher Scott (2018)
FP183 *Pondering, Praying, Preaching: Romans 8* Bonnie Thurston (2019, 2nd edn 2021)
FP184 *Shem`on the Graceful: Discourse on the Solitary Life* trans. with introd. Mary Hansbury (2020)
FP185 *God Under My Roof: Celtic Songs and Blessings* Esther de Waal (2020)
FP186 *Journeying with the Jesus Prayer* James F. Wellington (2020)
FP187 *Poet of the Word: Re-reading Scripture with Ephraem the Syrian* Aelred Partridge OC (2020)

FP188 *Identity and Ritual* Alan Griffiths (2021)
FP189 *River of the Spirit: The Spirituality of Simon Barrington-Ward* Andy Lord (2021)
FP190 *Prayer and the Struggle against Evil* John Barton, Daniel Lloyd, James Ramsay, Alexander Ryrie (2021)
FP191 *Dante's Spiritual Journey: A Reading of the Divine Comedy* Tony Dickinson (2021)
FP192 *Jesus the Undistorted Image of God* John Townroe (2022)
FP193 *Our Deepest Desire: Prayer, Fasting & Almsgiving in the Writings of Saint Augustine of Hippo* Sister Susan SLG (2022)
FP194 *Lent with George Herbert* Tony Dickinson (2022)
FP195 *Four Ways to the Cross* Tony Dickinson (2022)
FP196 *Anselm of Canterbury, Teacher of Prayer* Sister Benedicta Ward SLG (2022)
FP197 *With One Heart and Mind: Prayers out of Stillness* Anthony Kemp (2023)
FP198 *Sayings of the Urban Fathers & Mothers* James Ashdown (2023)
FP199 *Doors* Sister Raphael SLG (2023)
FP200 *Monastic Vocation* SISTERS OF THE LOVE OF GOD, Bishop Rowan Williams (2021)
FP201 *An Ecology of the Heart: Faith Through the Climate Crisis* Duncan Forbes (2023)
FP202 *'In the image of the Image': Gregory of Nyssa's Opposition to Slavery* Adam Couchman (2023)
FP203 *Gregory of Nyssa and the Sins of Asia Minor* Jonathan Farrugia (2023)
FP204 *Discovery* Arthur Bell (2023)
FP205 *Living Healing: the Spirituality of Leanne Payne* Andy Lord (2023)
FP206 *Still Listening: Sowing the Seeds of the Jesus Prayer* Bruce Batstone CJN (2023)
FP207 *Julian of Norwich: Four Essays to Commemorate 650 Years of The Revelations of Divine Love* Father Colin SWG, Mother Hilary Crupi OJN Sr Elizabeth Ruth Obbard OC, Bishop Graham Usher, (2023)
FP208 *Time* Dumitru Stăniloae, Kallistos Ware (2023)
FP209 *Pearls of Life: A Lifebelt for the Spirit* Tony Dickinson (2023)

CONTEMPLATIVE POETRY SERIES

CP1 *Amado Nervo: Poems of Faith and Doubt* trans. John Gallas (2021)
CP2 *Anglo-Saxon Poets: The High Roof of Heaven* trans. John Gallas (2021)
CP3 *Middle English Poets: Where Grace Grows Ever Green* ed. John Gallas (2021)
CP4 *Selected Poems: The Voice inside Our Home* Edward Clarke (2022)
CP5 *Women & God: Drops in the Sea of Time* trans. & ed. John Gallas (2022)
CP6 *Gabrielle de Coignard & Vittoria Colonna: Fly Not Too High* trans. John Gallas (2022)
CP7 *Selected Poems: Chancing on Sanctity* James Ramsay (2022)
CP8 *Gabriela Mistral: This Far Place* trans. John Gallas (2023)
CP9 *Henry Vaughan & George Herbert: Divine Themes and Celestial Praise* ed. Edward Clarke (2023)
CP10 *Love Will Come with Fire* SISTERS OF THE LOVE OF GOD (2023)
CP11 *Touchpapers* collected & trans. John Gallas (2023)
CP12 *Reinhard Sorge: Take Flight to God* trans. John Gallas (2023)

VESTRY GUIDES

VG1 *The Visiting Minister: How to Welcome Visiting Clergy to Your Church* Paul Monk (2021)
VG2 *Help! No Minister! or Please Take the Service* Paul Monk (2022)

slgpress.co.uk